MW00989506

HOMERIC VOCABULARIES

Greek and English Word-Lists
for the Study of Homer

BY

WILLIAM BISHOP OWEN

AND

EDGAR JOHNSON GOODSPEED

New Edition, Rearranged and Enlarged,
and with a Foreword,
by
CLYDE PHARR

UNIVERSITY OF OKLAHOMA PRESS : NORMAN

Library of Congress Catalog Card Number: 68-31669

ISBN 978-0-8061-0828-5 (paper)

FOREWORD

THE COURSE OF English literature might have been different if Keats, instead of looking into Chapman's Homer, could have looked into Homer in Homer's own language. Homer and the literature and thinking of his age continue to present a rewarding field for today's scholars, both young and old. This book is designed to make their efforts easier, to facilitate their understanding and mastery of the Homeric vocabulary.

An essential step in learning and using any language is the acquisition of a working vocabulary. Many methods have been devised to help with this acquisition, all of them stressing the fundamental importance of mastering the words most frequently used. The Owen and Goodspeed word-lists, in which Homeric terms are arranged according to frequency of usage, divided into categories according to parts of speech, and presented in an easy-to-use format, are particularly helpful.

The *Homeric Vocabularies* of Owen and Goodspeed has been used successfully by teachers and students over many years. If, during this long period of use, the book has had any major defect, it has been—according to today's students—the separation of the Greek words from their English meanings. In previous editions, the Greek list was in the first part of the book and the corresponding English list in the back part, an arrangement that, according to some, required unnecessary and occasionally frustrating labor. In this edition, the Greek word and its English meaning are shown on the same page. This arrangement and the addition of three indexes should make an important book even more useful.

CLYDE PHARR

Austin, Texas

PREFACE

THIS SERIES OF word-lists is the outgrowth of the conviction that the ordinary way of acquiring Homeric vocabulary is both wasteful and ineffectual. The chief difficulty in learning to read Homer lies in the large and varied character of the vocabulary required, and these lists have been prepared in order to help the student to learn Homeric words in a systematic and practical way. A moderate number of words learned each day and constantly reviewed will rapidly enlarge the student's working vocabulary, and steadily better his equipment for sight-reading. He will gradually be emancipated from the constant use of the lexicon, while his knowledge of Greek words will gain rather than lose in precision and permanence. Each day a few new words should be learned, and those previously learned should be rapidly reviewed. The student will very shortly find himself possessed of a vocabulary which will greatly facilitate the work of translation, and make the reading of Homer at sight a pleasant and natural exercise. In short, it is believed that the mastery of these lists will secure for the student that much-talked-of thing, the ability to read Homer; and make of his study of it a means, not simply of discipline, but of enjoyment and culture.

THE EDITORS

PREFACE TO THE SECOND EDITION

THE DEMAND FOR A new edition of these lists has given us the opportunity to correct some misprints and to modify a few definitions. The numberings remain unchanged throughout. Attention may be called to the fact that in the statistics of verb occurrences, compounds have been reckoned with their primitives. In this we have followed the procedure of Gehring's *Index Homericus,* upon the materials of which our statistics are based.

THE EDITORS

CONTENTS

Contents

HOMERIC VOCABULARIES

VERBS

List I
Verbs Occurring
500–2,000 Times

1	ἄγω	Lead
2	βαίνω	Go
3	βάλλω	Throw, smite
4	δίδωμι	Give
5	εἰμί	Am
6	εἶμι	Go
7	εἶπον	Spoke, said
8	ἔρχομαι	Come, go
9	ἔχω	Have
10	ἵστημι	Set, stand
11	ὁράω	See
12	τίθημι	Make, put
13	φημί	Say, declare

14	αἱρέω	Take, choose
15	ἀμείβω	Exchange, answer
16	αὐδάω	Speak
17	γίγνομαι	Become, am born
18	ἐθέλω	Will, wish
19	ἕπω	Move about, am busy; follow
20	ἵημι	Let go, send
21	ἱκνέομαι	Come to, reach
22	κεῖμαι	Lie, am placed
23	κτείνω	Kill
24	λείπω	Leave
25	μένω	Remain, await
26	οἶδα	Know
27	ὄλλυμι	Lose, destroy
28	ὄρνυμι	Arouse
29	πείθω	Persuade
30	πίπτω	Fall
31	φέρω	Bear, bring
32	φεύγω	Flee
33	φωνέω	Speak aloud
34	χέω	Pour, shed

35	ἀγορεύω	Harangue, speak
36	ἀΐσσω	Dart
37	ἀκούω	Hear
38	ἀμύνω	Ward off, defend, assist
39	ἀνώγω	Bid, command
40	ἄρχω	Begin, lead
41	γιγνώσκω	Come to know, know
42	δάμνημι	Subdue, tame
43	δείδω	Dread, fear
44	δέχομαι	Accept, receive
45	δύναμαι	Am able
46	δύω	Enter, put on
47	ἐάω	Let, permit
48	ἕζομαι	Sit down
49	εἴρω	Say, declare
50	ἐλάω	Strike, drive
51	ἔοικα	Am like, befit
52	ἐρύω	Draw, drag off
53	εὔχομαι	Pray, vow, declare
54	ἧμαι	Sit
55	θνῄσκω	Die, am killed
56	ἱκάνω	Arrive at, reach
57	καλέω	Call, summon
58	καλύπτω	Cover, hide
59	κελεύω	Urge, command
60	κίω	Go, go away
61	κλύω	Hearken
62	λαμβάνω	Take

63	λέγω	Gather, tell
64	λύω	Loose, release
65	μάχομαι	Fight
66	μέμαα	Am eager, press on
67	μιμνήσκω	Remind, recall
68	ναίω	Dwell, inhabit
69	νέομαι	Go, return
70	νοέω	Perceive, think
71	οἴχομαι	Depart, am gone
72	ὀίω	Think, expect
73	ὀτρύνω	Urge on
74	πάσχω	Suffer
75	παύω	Stop
76	πέλω	Am
77	πέμπω	Send, escort
78	πνείω	Breathe, am prudent
79	ῥέζω	Work, offer
80	σεύω	Start, drive; rush
81	τελέω	End, complete
82	τέρπω	Delight
83	τεύχω	Make
84	τίκτω	Bring forth, beget
85	τρέπω	Turn
86	φαίνω, φάω	Show, reveal
87	φράζομαι	Point out, show
88	φρονέω	Think, intend
89	χαίρω	Rejoice

7

90	ἀγείρω	Collect
91	ἅλλομαι	Leap
92	ἀνάσσω	Am king, rule
93	ἅπτω	Fasten, lay hold of
94	ἀραρίσκω	Fit together, fit
95	ἄχνυμαι	Grieve
96	δαίνυμι	Distribute, feast
97	δέω	Bind
98	ἐγείρω	Awake, arouse
99	ἔδω	Eat
100	εἴδομαι	See, seem
101	εἴρομαι	Ask, inquire
102	ἕλκω	Drag, draw
103	ἔλπω	Make hope, hope
104	ἕννυμι	Clothe
105	ἔρδω	Do, sacrifice
106	ἐρύκω	Hold back, restrain
107	εὕδω	Sleep
108	εὑρίσκω	Find
109	ζώω	Live
110	ἠμί	Say, speak
111	θέω	Run
112	ἵζω	Sit, cause to sit
113	ἴσχω	Hold, check
114	καίω	Burn, kindle
115	κέλομαι	Command, exhort
116	κιχάνω	Find, light upon
117	κλαίω	Weep

118	κλίνω	Lean, sink
119	κρίνώ	Separate, decide, select
120	λανθάνω	Escape, notice; forget (mid.)
121	λίσσομαι	Pray, entreat
122	μάρναμαι	Fight
123	μαχέομαι	Fight
124	μέλλω	Am going, am about
125	μέλω	Concern, interest
126	μίμνω	Remain, await
127	μίσγω, μίγνυμι	Mix, mingle
128	μυθέομαι	Relate, tell
129	νέμω	Distribute, pasture
130	νοστέω	Return
131	ὀδύρομαι	Lament
132	ὀνομάζω	Name
133	ὀπάζω	Attend, bestow
134	ὀρμάω	Set in motion; rush
135	ὀρούω	Spring
136	πειράω	Try
137	πέρθω	Sack, Waste
138	πέτομαι	Fly
139	πίμπλημι	Fill
140	πίνω	Drink
141	πλήσσω	Strike, smite
142	ποιέω	Make
143	πολεμίζω	War
144	πόρον	Bring to pass; give, grant
145	πυνθάνομαι	Learn, ascertain
146	ῥέω	Flow
147	ῥήγνυμι	Break
148	σαόω	Save
149	στρέφω	Turn, twist
150	τάμνω	Cut

151	τανύω	Stretch
152	ἐπιτέλλω	Enjoin, charge
153	τίω	Value, honor
154	τλάω	Endure
155	τρέφω	Nourish, rear
156	ἔπεφνον	Kill, slay
157	φθίνω	Waste away, perish
158	φιλέω	Love
159	φορέω	Bear, carry
160	χολόω	Enrage, anger
161	ὠθέω	Thrust, drive

162	ἀγγέλλω	Report, announce
163	ἄγνυμι	Break
164	ἀγοράομαι	Hold assembly, speak
165	ἀείδω	Sing
166	αἰδέομαι	Respect, scruple
167	αἰνέω	Praise
168	ἀκαχίζω	Distress, grieve
169	ἀκοντίζω	Hurl the javelin, hurl
170	ἀλάομαι	Wander, rove
171	ἀλεείνω	Shun, avoid
172	ἀλέξω	Ward off, defend, assist
173	ἀλεύομαι	Shun, avoid
174	ἀλύσκω	Shun, avoid
175	ἁμαρτάνω	Miss, err
176	ἁνδάνω	Please
177	ἀπαυράω	Rob, deprive
178	ἀπειλέω	Threaten, menace
179	ἀπιθέω	Disobey
180	ἀποαίνυμαι	Take away
181	ἀράομαι	Pray, wish, curse
182	ἄρνυμαι	Carry off, win
183	ἁρπάζω	Seize, snatch
184	αὔω	Call aloud
185	βοάω	Shout
186	βουλεύω	Deliberate, advise
187	βούλομαι	Will, wish
188	γαμέω	Marry
189	γείνομαι	Am born, bear, beget

190	γελόω	Laugh
191	γηθέω	Rejoice, am glad
192	γοάω	Wail
193	δαήσεαι	Teach, learn
194	δαίω	Kindle, blaze
195	δατέομαι	Divide
196	δείκνυμι	Show, point out
197	δεύομαι	Lack
198	διώκω	Pursue, speed
199	δοκέω	Think, seem
200	δουπέω	Thunder
201	δύνω	Enter, put on, set
202	ἐέργω, ἔργομαι	Shut off, shut in
203	εἴκω	Yield
204	εἴλω	Crowd together, hem in
205	ἐλαύνω	Drive, strike
206	ἐλεαίρω	Pity
207	ἐλεέω	Pity
208	ἐναρίζω	Despoil, slay
209	ἐνέπω	Relate
210	ἐπείγω	Press hard, impel
211	ἐπίσταμαι	Know how, understand
212	ἐρεείνω	Ask
213	ἐρείδω	Lean, press down
214	ἐρείπω	Overthrow, fall down
215	ἐρέω	Ask
216	ἐρίζω	Contend, strive
217	ἐσθίω	Eat
218	ἡγεμονεύω	Am leader, command
219	ἡγέομαι	Guide, lead
220	θαυμάζω	Wonder, admire
221	θρώσκω	Leap, spring up
222	θωρήσσω	Arm with cuirass
223	ἰάλλω	Send

224	ἰάχω	Cry, shriek
225	ἱερεύω	Sacrifice, slaughter
226	ἰθύνω	Make straight, direct
227	ἵκω	Reach
228	κάμνω	Work, grow weary
229	κείρω	Shear, cut down
230	κεύθω	Hide, cover
231	κήδω	Distress; care for
232	κοιμάω	Put to rest, lull
233	κομίζω	Wait upon, convey
234	κόπτω	Knock, smite
235	κορύσσω	Arm with helmet, arm
236	κυλίνδω	Roll
237	λαγχάνω	Obtain by lot, receive
238	λάμπω	Shine
239	λήγω	Cease, abate
240	λήθω	Escape notice
241	λούω	Bathe, wash
242	μενεαίνω	Eagerly desire, am angered, strive
243	μερμηρίζω	Ponder
244	μεταλλάω	Search after, question
245	μήδομαι	Take counsel, devise
246	μνάομαι	Woo
247	μογέω	Toil, suffer
248	ναιετάω	Am situated, inhabit
249	νεικέω	Strive, quarrel, upbraid
250	νεμεσάω	Am angry, take it ill
251	νεύω	Nod
252	νικάω	Conquer
253	νύσσω	Prick, pierce
254	νωμάω	Deal out, wield
255	ὀλοφύρομαι	Bewail
256	ὄμνυμι	Take oath
257	ὁπλίζω	Equip, prepare

258	ὀρέγνυμι	Reach, extend
259	ὀρίνω	Rouse, move
260	ὁρμαίνω	Debate, ponder
261	οὐτάζω	Stab, wound
262	οὐτάω	Stab, wound
263	ὀφείλω	Owe, ought
264	ὀχθέω	Am moved, vexed
265	παπταίνω	Peer about
266	πελάζω	Bring near
267	περάω	Pass through, traverse
268	πήγνυμι	Fix, build
269	πλάζω	Strike, drive back; wander
270	πλέω	Sail
271	πονέομαι	Labor, am busy
272	πρήσσω	Pass over, accomplish
273	σπένδω	Pour, make a libation
274	στενάχω	Groan, lament
275	τείνω	Stretch
276	τείρω	Wear out, weary
277	τελευτάω	End, complete
278	τιμάω	Prize, honor
279	τίνω	Atone for, pay
280	τρέχω	Run
281	τυγχάνω	Hit, happen
282	τύπτω	Strike, hit
283	φθάνω	Am before, anticipate
284	φοβέω	Put to flight
285	φυλάσσω	Watch, guard
286	φύω	Make grow, grow
287	χάζομαι	Give way, give over, deprive
288	χαρίζω	Show favor, gratify
289	χώομαι	Am troubled, angered
290	χωρέω	Give place, withdraw

291	ἀάω	Delude, beguile
292	ἄγαμαι	Admire, am indignant
293	ἀέξω	Make to grow, increase
294	ἄημι	Blow
295	αἴδομαι	Feel shame, reverence
296	αἰσχύνω	Disgrace, insult
297	αἰτέω	Ask, demand
298	αἰτίζω	Beg, importune
299	ἀίω	Hear, perceive
300	ἀκέομαι	Heal
301	ἀλαπάζω	Empty, sack
302	ἀλέγω	Care, am concerned for
303	ἀλείφω	Anoint
304	ἀλίσκομαι	Am taken, captured
305	ἀμάω	Mow, reap
306	ἀναίνομαι	Deny, refuse
307	ἀντάω	Meet, encounter
308	ἀντιάω	Encounter, take part in
309	ἀντιβολέω	Encounter, take part in
310	ἀντιόω	Encounter, take part in
311	ἄντομαι	Meet, encounter
312	ἀνύω	Accomplish
313	ἀπατάω	Deceive
314	ἀραβέω	Clatter
315	ἀράσσω	Pound, shatter
316	ἀρέσκω	Make amends
317	ἀρήγω	Aid, support
318	ἀριστεύω	Am the best, bravest

319	ἀρκέω	Protect, help
320	ἀρνέομαι	Deny, decline
321	ἀρτύνω	Put in order, arrange
322	ἀσκέω	Work out
323	ἀσπαίρω	Quiver
324	ἀτιμάζω	Dishonor, maltreat
325	ἀτιμάω	Dishonor, maltreat
326	ἀτιτάλλω	Rear, cherish
327	ἀτύζομαι	Am dazed, bewildered
328	ἀφύσσω	Draw, dip
329	ἀχεύω	Grieve
330	ἄω	Satiate
331	βάζω	Talk, speak
332	βασιλεύω	Am king
333	βιάω	Force, constrain
334	βλάπτω	Impede, arrest, harm
335	βόσκω	Feed, pasture
336	βράχω	Rattle, creak, roar
337	βρίθω	Am heavy, charge
338	γέγωνα	Make myself heard, cry out
339	γνάμπτω	Bend
340	γουνόομαι	Supplicate, implore
341	δαΐζω	Cleave, slay
342	δακρύω	Shed tears, weep
343	δάμνημι	Tame, subdue
344	δειπνέω	Take a meal
345	δέμω	Build, construct
346	δέρκομαι	Look, see
347	δέρω	Flay
348	δεύω	Wet, moisten
349	δηλέομαι	Harm, slay, waste
350	δηόω, δηιόω	Slay, destroy
351	διδάσκω	Teach

352	δίεμαι	Am scared away, flee
353	δίζημαι	Go to seek, seek to win
354	δινέω	Whirl
355	δοάσσατο	Seem, appear
356	ἐγγυαλίζω	Hand over, confer
357	ἐέλδομαι, ἔλδομαι	Desire, long for
358	ἔθω	Am wont
359	εἴβω	Shed, let fall
360	εἰλύω	Wrap, envelop
361	εἰρύομαι	Drag, rescue
362	ἐΐσκω	Make like, compare to
363	ἐλελίζω	Set quaking, whirl round
364	ἑλίσσω	Curl, wind
365	ἐμπάζομαι	Care for
366	ἐναίρω	Slay
367	ἐνίπτω	Chide
368	ἐντύνω	Make ready, adorn
369	ἐπαυρίσκω	Acquire, enjoy
370	ἐρέσσω	Row
371	ἐρητύω	Restrain, control
372	ἔρρω	Go (painfully)
373	ἔρυμαι	Shield, protect
374	ἐρωέω	Flow, recede
375	ἔσθω	Eat
376	εὐνάω	Place in ambush, lay to rest
377	εὐχετάομαι	Pray, boast
378	ἐχθαίρω	Hate
379	ζεύγνυμι	Yoke
380	ζώννυμι	Gird
381	ἡβάω	Am at my youthful prime
382	θαμβέω	Wonder at
383	θάπτω	Bury
384	θαρσέω	Am bold

385	θαρσύνω	Encourage
386	θείνω	Strike
387	θέλγω	Enchant
388	θηέομαι	Gaze at, behold
389	θύνω	Rush on, charge
390	θύω	Offer (as burnt offering)
391	ἰαίνω	Warm, cheer; delight in
392	ἰαύω	Sleep, lodge
393	ἰθύω	Advance, attack
394	καθαίρω	Cleanse
395	καίνυμαι	Excel
396	κεάζω	Split, cleave
397	κεδάννυμι	Scatter
398	κείω	Wish to sleep
399	κεράννυμι	Mix
400	κερτομέω	Taunt, tease
401	κικλήσκω	Call, summon
402	κινέω	Move, stir
403	κλάζω	Scream, ring
404	κλάω	Break
405	κλονέω	Put to rout
406	κοιρανέω	Am lord, rule
407	κορέω (fut.)	Sate, satisfy
408	κοσμέω	Arrange, marshal
409	κοτέω	Am angry with
410	κραιαίνω	Accomplish, fulfill
411	κρατέω	Am superior, rule over
412	κρύπτω	Hide, conceal
413	κυκάω	Stir up, mix up
414	κυνέω	Kiss
415	κωκύω	Wail
416	λάζομαι	Take
417	λείβω	Pour, shed

418	λεύσσω	See, behold
419	λιάζομαι	Turn aside, withdraw
420	λιλαίομαι	Desire
421	λοέω	Bathe, wash
422	λοχάω	Lie in ambush
423	μαίνομαι	Am mad, rage
424	μαίομαι	Seek for, explore
425	μαντεύομαι	Divine, prophesy
426	μάρπτω	Seize, overtake
427	μαστίζω	Lash, whip
428	μέδομαι	Bethink myself of, devise
429	μειδάω	Smile
430	μέμονα	Have in mind, am prompted
431	μενοινώω	Ponder, intend
432	μηνίω	Am wroth
433	μητιάω	Deliberate, devise
434	μηχανάω	Contrive, perpetrate
435	μιστύλλω	Cut in small pieces
436	μύρομαι	Flow, weep
437	νεικείω	Quarrel, upbraid
438	νήχω	Swim
439	νίζω	Wash, wash off
440	νίπτω	Wash, wash off
441	νίσομαι, νίσσομαι	Go, come, return
442	νοσφίζομαι	Depart from, hold aloof
443	ξεινίζω	Receive, entertain
444	οἴγνυμι	Open
445	οἰμώζω	Cry out, lament
446	ὀιστεύω	Shoot an arrow
447	ὀλέκω	Lose, destroy
448	ὁμιλέω	Throng about, go with
449	ὁμοκλάω, -έω	Shout together, command
450	ὁμόργνυμι	Wipe away

451	ὀνίνημι	Help
452	ὄνομαι	Scorn
453	ὀνομαίνω	Name, mention
454	ὀπτάω	Roast
455	ὀπυίω	Wed, take to wife
456	ὄσσομαι	See, threaten
457	ὀφέλλω	Increase
458	ὀχέω	Bear, endure
459	παλάσσω	Sprinkle, defile
460	παμφανόω	Shine, gleam
461	πατέομαι	Taste, enjoy
462	πεδάω	Fetter, constrain
463	πειρητίζω	Test
464	πείρω	Pierce, transfix
465	πελεμίζω	Shake, brandish
466	πένομαι	Labor over, prepare
467	πετάννυμι	Spread out
468	πιφαύσκω	Make manifest, make to shine
469	ποθέω	Miss, yearn for
470	πρέπω	Am conspicuous
471	πρήθω	Blow, stream, burn
472	προβλώσκω	Come forth, go forth
473	πτύσσω	Fold
474	πτώσσω	Cower, hide
475	πυκάζω	Cover closely, wrap up
476	πωλέομαι	Frequent, consort with
477	ῥαίω	Shatter, dash
478	ῥιγέω	Shudder
479	ῥίπτω	Fling, hurl
480	ῥύομαι	Rescue, save
481	ῥώομαι	Move quickly
482	σείω	Shake, brandish
483	σημαίνω	Command, point out

484	σκεδάννυμι	Scatter, disperse
485	σκίδναμαι	Scatter, disperse
486	σπάω	Pull, draw
487	σπέρχω	Speed, drive fast
488	σπεύδω	Am quick, hasten
489	στείχω	March, move
490	στέλλω	Make ready, send off
491	στεναχίζω	Sigh, groan
492	στορέννυμι	Spread, lay
493	στρωφάω	Turn constantly, dwell
494	στυγέω	Loathe, hate
495	στυφελίζω	Smite, knock about
496	συλάω	Despoil
497	σφάζω	Slaughter
498	ταρβέω	Am afraid, dread
499	τέθηπα	Am amazed at
500	τελέθω	Am become, be
501	τετίημαι	Am troubled
502	τήκω	Melt
503	τινάσσω	Shake, brandish
504	τιταίνω	Stretch, draw
505	τιτύσκομαι	Aim, prepare
506	τμήγω	Cut, separate
507	τολμάω	Endure, dare
508	τρέω	Flee, fear
509	τρίβω	Rub, wear out
510	τρομέω	Tremble, quake, dread
511	τρύχω	Exhaust, consume
512	τρωπάω	Turn, change
513	ὑφαίνω	Weave
514	φαείνω	Shine
515	φέβομαι	Flee, flee from
516	φείδομαι	Spare

517	φθέγγομαι	Utter a sound, speak out
518	φθινύθω	Waste away, pine
519	φθονέω	Grudge, deny
520	φοιτάω	Go to and fro, roam
521	φυτεύω	Plant, plan
522	χαλεπαίνω	Rage, am angry
523	χανδάνω	Hold, contain
524	χραισμέω	Help, ward off
525	χράομαι	Have use of, need of
526	χρίω	Anoint

NOUNS

List VII
Nouns Occurring
500–1000 Times

1	ἀνήρ	Man
2	θεός	God
3	θυμός	Heart, soul, life
4	νηῦς	Ship
5	υἱός	Son
6	χείρ	Hand

7	ἄναξ	Lord, king
8	γαῖα	Earth, land
9	γέρων	Old man
10	γυνή	Woman
11	δόρυ	Beam, tree, spear
12	δῶμα	House, room
13	ἔγχος	Spear, lance
14	ἔπος	Word
15	ἔργον	Work, deed, thing
16	ἕταρος, ἕταιρος	Companion
17	ἵππος	Horse
18	λαός	People, host
19	μέγαρον	Hall, dining-hall
20	μήτηρ	Mother
21	μνηστήρ	Suitor
22	μῦθος	Word, saying
23	ξεῖνος	Stranger, guest, host
24	παῖς	Child
25	πατήρ	Father
26	πόλεμος	War, battle
27	πόλις	City
28	πούς	Foot
29	φρήν	Diaphragm, mind
30	χαλκός	Copper, bronze

31	αἷμα	Blood
32	ἄλοχος	Wife
33	ἅλς	Salt (m.), sea (f.)
34	ἄνεμος	Wind
35	ἄνθρωπος	Man
36	ἄστυ	City
37	βασιλεύς	King
38	βίη	Force, violence
39	βοῦς	Cow, ox
40	γόνυ	Knee
41	δάκρυ	Tear
42	δῆμος	People
43	δόμος	House, home
44	δῶρον	Gift
45	ἠέλιος	Sun
46	ἦμαρ	Day
47	ἥρως	Hero, warrior
48	ἠώς	Dawn, morning
49	θάλασσα	Sea
50	θάνατος	Death
51	θεά	Goddess
52	κεφαλή	Head
53	κλισίη	Hut
54	κούρη	Young girl, daughter
55	κῦμα	Wave
56	κύων	Dog
57	μάχη	Fight
58	μένος	Might

59	μοῖρα	Part, fate
60	νόος	Mind, thought
61	νύξ	Night
62	οἶκος	House
63	οἶνος	Wine
64	ὀφθαλμός	Eye
65	πεδίον	Plain
66	πόντος	Sea, deep
67	ποταμός	River
68	πῦρ	Fire
69	στῆθος	Breast
70	τεῖχος	Wall
71	τεῦχος	Arms, armor, tackle
72	τόξον	Bow
73	ὕδωρ	Water
74	ὕπνος	Sleep
75	χρώς	Skin, body
76	ὦμος	Shoulder

77	ἀγορή	Assembly, speech
78	αἴξ	Goat
79	ἄλγος	Pain
80	ἀλκή	Defense, valor
81	ἀμφίπολος	Handmaid
82	ἄρμα	Chariot
83	ἀσπίς	Shield
84	ἄχος	Anguish
85	βέλος	Missile
86	βοή	Shout
87	βούλη	Counsel, plan
88	γόος	Lamentation
89	γυῖα (pl.)	Joints, limbs
90	δαίμων	Divinity
91	δαίς	Feast
92	δέπας	Goblet
93	δίφρος	Chariot, stool
94	δμωή	Female slave
95	εἶμα	Garment
96	εὐνή	Bed, anchor
97	ἦτορ	Heart
98	θάλαμος	Chamber
99	θεράπων	Comrade-at-arms
100	θρόνος	Arm chair
101	θύρη	Door, gate
102	κάρη	Head
103	κήρ	Death, fate
104	κῆρ	Heart

105	κῆρυξ	Herald
106	κλέος	Rumor, glory
107	κονίη	Dust, ashes
108	κραδίη	Heart
109	κτῆμα	Possession, property
110	κῦδος	Glory, majesty
111	λέων	Lion
112	μῆλον	Sheep, goat
113	νέκυς	Corpse
114	νῆσος	Island
115	νόστος	Return
116	ξίφος	Sword
117	ὁδός	Way, journey
118	ὄις	Sheep
119	ὀιστός	Arrow
120	ὄλεθρος	Destruction
121	ὅμιλος	Throng
122	ὄρος	Mountain
123	ὄσσε	Eyes
124	οὐρανός	Heaven
125	ὄχος	Car, chariot
126	πέτρη	Rock, cliff
127	ποιμήν	Shepherd
128	πόνος	Labor, toil
129	πόσις	Husband, spouse
130	πότνια	Mistress, queen
131	πύλη	Gate
132	σάκος	Shield
133	σῆμα	Sign, token
134	σῖτος	Wheat, food
135	στρατός	Host, army
136	συβώτης	Swineherd
137	σῦς	Swine

138	τέκνον	Child
139	τέκος	Child
140	φάος	Light
141	φιλότης	Love, friendship
142	φώς	Man
143	χθών	Earth, ground
144	χιτών	Tunic
145	χλαίνη	Cloak, mantle
146	χόλος	Gall, wrath
147	χρή	Need
148	χρυσός	Gold
149	ψυχή	Life, soul

150	ἀγγελίη	Tidings
151	ἄγγελος	Messenger
152	ἀγρός	Field, country
153	ἀγών	Assemblage, game, arena
154	ἄεθλον	Prize
155	ἄεθλος	Contest
156	ἀήρ	Air
157	αἶα	Earth, land
158	αἰδώς	Shame, respect
159	αἰθήρ	Sky, upper air
160	αἶσα	Lot, destiny
161	αἰχμή	Point, spear
162	αἰχμητής	Spearman, warrior
163	ἀνάγκη	Necessity, constraint
164	ἀοιδή	Song
165	ἀοιδός	Bard
166	ἄποινα	Ransom
167	Ἀργειφόντης	Argeiphontes
168	ἀρετή	Excellence
169	ἄρης	Battle, combat
170	ἀριστεύς	Chief
171	ἄρνα	Lamb, sheep
172	ἄρουρα	Plough-land, ground
173	ἀρχός	Leader
174	ἄτη	Ruin, folly
175	αὐλή	Courtyard
176	αὐτή	Cry, call
177	αὐχήν	Neck

178	βίοτος	Life, substance
179	βλέφαρον	Eyelid
180	βορέης	North-wind
181	γάμος	Marriage
182	γαστήρ	Belly, womb
183	γενεή	Birth, race
184	γένος	Family, race
185	γέρας	Gift of honor, honor
186	γῆρας	Old age
187	δεῖπνον	Meal, repast
188	δέμας	Frame, build
189	δεσμός	Fetter, fastening
190	δηιοτής	Conflict
191	δμώς	Slave
192	δόλος	Deceit
193	δόρπον	Supper
194	ἐδητύς	Food
195	ἔθνος	Host, swarm, herd
196	εἶδος	Appearance
197	ἑκατόμβη	Hecatomb
198	ἔλαιον	Olive-oil
199	ἐνιαυτός	Year
200	ἔντεα	Armor, weapons
201	ἐπίκουρος	Helper in battle
202	ἐρετμόν	Oar
203	ἔρις	Strife
204	ἔρκος	Hedge, wall, court
205	ἔρος	Love
206	ζυγόν	Yoke, crossbar
207	ἡγεμών	Guide, leader
208	ἡγήτωρ	Leader, chief
209	ἡμίονος	Mule
210	ἡνία	Reins

211	ἡνίοχος	Charioteer
212	ἤπειρος	Land, mainland
213	θέμις	Law, right
214	θίς	Heap, strand
215	θώρηξ	Breast-plate, cuirass
216	ἰός	Arrow
217	ἱππεύς	Chariot-man
218	ἱππότα	Horseman, knight
219	ἱρόν, ἱερόν	Sacrifice, victim
220	ἴς	Sinew, strength
221	ἱστός	Mast, loom
222	κακότης	Evil, cowardice
223	κάματος	Fatigue, toil
224	κασίγνητος	Brother
225	κέλευθος	Path
226	κῆδος	Care, mourning
227	κληίς	Bolt, collarbone, tholepin
228	κόρυς	Helmet
229	κορυφή	Crest
230	κοῦρος	Youth
231	κράτος	Strength, mastery
232	κρατός (gen.)	Head (gen.)
233	κρέας	Flesh, meat
234	κρητήρ	Mixing-bowl
235	κυνέη	Cap, helmet
236	λέχος	Couch, bed
237	λίθος	Stone
238	λιμήν	Harbor
239	μέδων	Ruler, counsellor
240	μηρός	Thigh
241	μῆτις	Counsel, plan
242	νεῖκος	Quarrel
243	νεφεληγερέτα	Cloud-gatherer

244	νέφος	Cloud
245	νίκη	Victory
246	νύμφη	Bride, lady
247	νῶτον	Back
248	ὀδούς	Tooth
249	ὀδύνη	Pain
250	οἰωνός	Bird of prey
251	ὅρκιον	Oath, victim
252	ὅρκος	Witness, oath
253	ὅρνις	Bird
254	ὄρχαμος	Leader
255	ὀστέον	Bone
256	οὔατος (gen.)	Ear (gen.)
257	οὖδας	Earth, floor
258	οὐδός	Threshold
259	ὄψ	Voice
260	πένθος	Mourning, grief
261	πῆμα	Woe, harm
262	πομπή	Dismissal, escort
263	πόσις	Drink
264	πότμος	Fate, death
265	πρόμαχος	Champion
266	πτόλεμος	War, battle
267	πτολίεθρον	Town, citadel
268	πτόλις	City
269	πύργος	Tower
270	πυρή	Pyre
271	ῥόος	Stream
272	σθένος	Strength
273	σίδηρος	Iron
274	σκῆπτρον	Staff, scepter
275	σπέος	Cave
276	σταθμός	Pen, fold, post

277	στίξ	Row, rank
278	στόμα	Mouth
279	τάφρος	Ditch
280	τέλος	End, completion
281	τιμή	Price, penalty, honor
282	τοκεύς	Parent, ancestor
283	τράπεζα	Table
284	τρίπος	Tripod
285	ὕλη	Wood, forest
286	ὑσμίνη	Conflict
287	φάλαγξ	Line of battle
288	φάρμακον	Herb, drug
289	φᾶρος	Cloak
290	φάσγανον	Sword
291	φόβος	Flight
292	φόνος	Murder
293	φωνή	Voice
294	χρόνος	Time
295	χῶρος	Space, place
296	ὥρη	Season, time

297	ἀγός	Leader
298	ἄγυια	Road, way
299	ἀδελφεός	Brother
300	ἀέθλιον	Prize
301	ἄελλα	Gust
302	αἰγίς	Aegis
303	αἰετός	Eagle
304	αἴθουσα	Portico, corridor
305	αἰπόλος	Goat-herd
306	αἰών	Life-time, life
307	ἄκοιτις	Wife
308	ἀκτή	Shore
309	ἀκωκή	Point
310	ἀλήτης	Vagabond
311	ἀλοιφή	Ointment
312	ἄλφιτον	Barley
313	ἀλωή	Threshing-floor, vineyard
314	ἄμαξα	Wagon
315	ἀμβροσίη	Ambrosia
316	ἄνθος	Blossom, flower
317	ἄντρον	Cave
318	ἄντυξ	Rim
319	ἄορ	Sword
320	ἀπήνη	Wagon
321	ἄργυρος	Silver
322	ἀρή	Prayer, curse
323	ἀρχή	Beginning
324	ἀσπιστής	Warrior

325	ἀστήρ	Star
326	ἀτασθαλίη	Folly
327	αὐγή	Gleam, glow
328	αὐδή	Voice
329	ἀυτμή	Breath, blast
330	ἀφραδίη	Ignorance, folly
331	ἀχλύς	Mist, darkness
332	βασίλεια	Queen
333	βένθος	Depth
334	βῆσσα	Glen, ravine
335	βιός	Bow
336	βουκόλος	Herdsman
337	βωμός	Step, platform, altar
338	γαμβρός	Son-in-law, brother-in-law
339	γῆ	Earth, land
340	γλῶσσα	Tongue, language
341	γόνος	Birth, offspring
342	γρηῦς	Old woman
343	δαΐς	Torch
344	δάπεδον	Ground, pavement
345	δειρή	Neck, throat
346	δέμνιον	Bedstead, bed
347	δένδρεον	Tree
348	δέος	Fear
349	δέρμα	Skin, hide
350	δέσποινα	Mistress
351	δημός	Fat
352	διάκτωρ	Runner, guide
353	δίκη	Usage, justice
354	δοῦπος	Din, thunder
355	δρόμος	Race, racecourse
356	δρῦς	Tree, oak
357	δύναμις	Power, strength

358	δῶ	House, room
359	ἐγκέφαλος	Brain
360	ἐγχείη	Lance
361	ἕδος	Seat, abode
362	ἕδρη	Seat
363	ἐδωδή	Food
364	ἐέλδωρ	Desire, wish
365	εἶδαρ	Food
366	εἴδωλον	Shape, phantom
367	ἐλαίη	Olive-tree
368	ἔλαφος	Stag
369	ἐλέφας	Ivory
370	ἕλκος	Wound, sore
371	ἔναρα (pl.)	Spoils
372	ἔπαλξις	Battlement
373	Ἐρινύς	Erinys
374	ἐρωή	Rush, sweep
375	ἐσθής	Clothing
376	ἐσχάρη	Hearth
377	ἐσχατιή	Border, edge
378	ἔτος	Year
379	εὖχος	Glory
380	εὐχωλή	Prayer, boast
381	ἐφετμή	Command
382	ζέφυρος	West-wind
383	ζόφος	Darkness, evening
384	ζωστήρ	Girdle
385	ἥβη	Youth
386	ἠιών	Shore
387	ἠχή	Noise, roar
388	θάρσος	Courage, boldness
389	θαῦμα	Wonder
390	θήρ	Wild beast

391	θρῆνυς	Foot-stool
392	θρίξ	Hair
393	θύελλα	Blast, gust
394	ἰαχή	Cry, shriek
395	ἱδρώς	Sweat
396	ἱκέτης	Suppliant
397	ἴκρια (pl.)	Deck, ribs
398	ἱμάς	Strap, thong
399	ἵμερος	Longing
400	ἰότης	Will
401	ἱππηλάτα	Chariot-fighter, knight
402	ἱστίον	Sail
403	ἰχθύς	Fish
404	κάλλος	Beauty
405	κάνεον	Basket
406	καπνός	Smoke
407	κάπρος	Boar
408	κάρηνα	Heads, summits
409	καρπός	Fruit, grain
410	καρπός	Wrist
411	κάρτος	Might, mastery
412	κασιγνήτη	Sister
413	κασσίτερος	Tin
414	κειμήλιον	Treasure, heirloom
415	κέρας	Horn
416	κεραυνός	Thunder-bolt, lightning
417	κέρδος	Gain, shrewdness
418	κίων	Pillar
419	κλῆρος	Lot, estate
420	κλισμός	Easy-chair
421	κνέφας	Darkness, dusk
422	κνήμη	Shin
423	κνίση	Savor, fat

39

424	κοῖτος	Sleep, resting place
425	κόλπος	Bosom, fold
426	κόμη	Hair
427	κόσμος	Order, ornament
428	κρήδεμνον	Head-band
429	κρήνη	Spring, fountain
430	κρόταφος	Temple (human)
431	κτέαρ	Possession, property
432	κτῆσις	Property
433	κτύπος	Crash, thunder
434	κύπελλον	Cup
435	κῶας	Fleece
436	λᾶας	Stone
437	λαῖλαψ	Tempest
438	λέβης	Caldron, basin
439	λειμών	Meadow
440	λέκτρον	Bed
441	ληΐς	Booty
442	λίμνη	Lake
443	λοιγός	Destruction, ruin
444	λόφος	Crest
445	λόχος	Ambush
446	λώβη	Insult
447	μάζος	Breast
448	μαῖα	Good mother
449	μάντις	Seer
450	μάστιξ	Whip
451	μέγεθος	Stature
452	μείς, μήν	Month
453	μελίη	Ash-tree, shaft, lance
454	μέλος	Limb, member
455	μετάφρενον	Back
456	μέτρον	Measure

457	μέτωπον	Forehead, front
458	μήδεα (pl.)	Plans, counsels
459	μῆνις	Wrath
460	μηρία (pl.)	Thigh-pieces
461	μήστωρ	Counsellor
462	μητίετα	Counsellor
463	μόρος	Lot, fate
464	μοῦσα	Muse
465	μυχός	Innermost part, corner
466	ναύτης	Sailor
467	νεβρός	Fawn
468	νευρή	Sinew, bowstring
469	νεφέλη	Cloud
470	νηός	Temple
471	νόημα	Thought, plan
472	νομεύς	Shepherd
473	νότος	South-wind
474	ξείνιον	Friendly gift
475	ξύλον	Wood, trunk
476	ὄβελος	Spit
477	ὄζος	Shoot, twig
478	ὀιζύς	Woe
479	οἰκία (pl.)	Abode
480	οἶτος	Fate
481	ὄλβος	Fortune, happiness
482	ὄμαδος	Din
483	ὄμβρος	Rain
484	ὀμηλικίη	Equal age, companion
485	ὄμμα	Eye
486	ὄνειαρ	Help, refreshment
487	ὄνειδος	Reproach
488	ὄνειρος	Dream
489	ὄνομα, οὔνομα	Name

490	ὅπλον	Rope, implement, arms
491	ὀρυμαγδός	Din
492	οὖρος	Fair wind
493	ὀφρύς	Brow
494	ὀχεύς	Holder
495	ὄχθη	Bank
496	παλάμη	Palm, hand
497	παράκοιτις	Wife
498	παρειά	Cheek
499	πάτρη	Native land
500	πέδιλα (pl.)	Sandals
501	πεῖραρ	End, cord
502	πέλεκυς	Axe
503	πέπλος	Robe
504	πληθύς	Multitude
505	πνοιή	Breath, blast
506	ποθή	Yearning, lack
507	ποινή	Penalty, price
508	πολεμιστής	Warrior
509	πομπός	Escort
510	ποτόν	Drink
511	πραπίς	Diaphragm, heart
512	πρόθυρον	Doorway, porch
513	πρόσωπον	Face
514	πρυμνήσιον	Stern-cable
515	πτερόν	Feather, wing
516	πῶυ	Flock
517	ῥάβδος	Rod, wand
518	ῥάκος	Ragged garment
519	ῥέεθρον	Stream, current
520	ῥηγμίς	Surf
521	ῥῆγος	Rug, blanket
522	ῥινός	Skin, shield

523	ῥίς	Nose, nostril
524	ῥοή	Flood, stream
525	σανίς	Board, plank, door
526	σέλας	Gleam
527	σίαλος	Fat hog
528	σκόπελος	Cliff
529	σκοπιή	Lookout, watch
530	σκοπός	Watchman
531	σκότος	Darkness
532	σπουδή	Effort, eagerness
533	στέρνον	Breast, chest
534	στοναχή	Groaning
535	σχεδίη	Raft, boat
536	τάλαντον	Scale, balance, talent
537	ταμίη	Housekeeper, stewardess
538	τάπης	Rug, coverlet
539	ταῦρος	Bull
540	τέκτων	Builder, carpenter
541	τελαμών	Strap, belt
542	τέμενος	Estate, precinct
543	τέρας	Prodigy
544	τοῖχος	Wall, side
545	τρόμος	Trembling, terror
546	τροφός	Nurse
547	τρυφάλεια	Helmet
548	τύμβος	Mound, tomb
549	ὕβρις	Insolence, violence
550	ὑπερώιον	Upper chamber
551	ὗς	Swine
552	ὑφορβός	Swineherd
553	φαρέτρη	Quiver
554	φλόξ	Flame, blaze
555	φόρμιγξ	Lute, lyre

43

556	φυή	Form
557	φύλλον	Leaf
558	φῦλον	Race, host
559	φύλοπις	Combat
560	χαίτη	Hair, mane
561	χάρις	Grace, charm
562	χάρμη	Joy of battle
563	χεῖλος	Lip, rim
564	χερμάδιον	Stone
565	χέρσος	Land, shore
566	χορός	Dancing place, dance
567	χρειώ	Want, need
568	χρεώ	Want, need
569	χρῆμα	Possession, property
570	ψάμαθος	Sand
571	ψεῦδος	Falsehood
572	ὠτειλή	Wound

PRONOUNS
ADJECTIVES
ADVERBS
PREPOSITIONS, ETC.

1	ἀλλά	But
2	ἄλλος	Other, another
3	ἄρα	So then
4	αὐτάρ	But, however
5	αὐτός	Same, self
6	γάρ	For, namely
7	γέ	At least
8	δέ	But, and
9	δή	Now indeed, really
10	ἐγώ	I
11	εἰ	If
12	εἰς, ἐς	Into
13	ἐκ, ἐξ	Out, out of
14	ἐν, ἐνί	In
15	ἔνθα	There, where
16	ἐπεί	When, since
17	ἐπί	Upon, on
18	ἤ, ἠέ	Or, than, whether
19	ἦ	In truth; pray? (affirmative or interrogative)
20	ἠδέ	And
21	καί	And, also
22	κατά, κάδ	Down
23	κέ	(Anticipatory or potential particle)
24	μάλα	Very, quite
25	μέγας	Great, large

26	μέν	Indeed
27	μή	Not, lest
28	μίν	Him, her, it
29	νῦν	Now
30	ὁ, ἡ, τό	This, he, the, who
31	ὅς, ἥ, ὅ	He, this, who
32	ὅτε	When, since
33	οὐ, οὐκ	Not
34	οὗ	Him, her
35	οὐδέ	Nor, not even
36	παρά	Beside, by
37	πᾶς	Every, all
38	περ	Very, at least
39	πολλός	Much, many
40	σύ	Thou
41	τὶς, τὶ	Someone, anyone
42	φίλος	Dear, own
43	ὡς	As, how, when, that
44	ὥς, ὣς	Thus, so

45	ἀθάνατος	Deathless, immortal
46	ἅμα	At the same time
47	ἀμφί	On both sides, about
48	ἄν	(Anticipatory or potential particle)
49	ἀνά	Up
50	ἀπό	From
51	ἄριστος	Best
52	αὖτε	Again, but
53	διά	Through
54	δῖος	Divine, glorious
55	ἕκαστος	Each
56	ἐμός	My, mine
57	ἑός	His, her, own
58	ἔπειτα	Thereupon, then
59	ἔτι	Still, yet
60	εὖ	Well
61	ἡμεῖς	We
62	κακός	Bad, cowardly
63	καλός	Beautiful, fine
64	μετά	Among, after
65	ὅδε	This
66	ὅσος	How great, how many
67	ὅς τε	Who
68	οὔτε	Neither, nor
69	οὗτος	This, that

70	ὄφρα	While, until
71	περί	Around, about
72	ποτέ	Ever, once
73	πρός, προτί, ποτί	Thereto, to, toward
74	σός	Thy, thine
75	σύν	Along with, with
76	σφεῖς	Themselves
77	τότε	Then, at that time
78	ὑπό	Under
79	ὤ, ὦ	O, oh!

80	ἀγαθός	Good
81	αἴ	If, whether
82	αἰεί	Always, ever
83	αἶψα	Forthwith
84	ἀλλήλων	One another, each other
85	ἀμύμων	Blameless
86	ἀμφοτέρω	Both
87	ἅπας	All
88	ἀτάρ	But
89	αὖ	Again, on the other hand
90	αὐτίκα	Straightway
91	αὖτις	Again, back again
92	ἄψ	Back
93	βροτός	Mortal
94	δύο, δύω	Two
95	ἐνθάδε	Hither, here
96	ἐσθλός	Good
97	εὐρύς	Broad
98	ἤδη	Already, now
99	θοός	Swift
100	ἵνα	Where, in order that
101	κεῖνος	That, that one, he
102	κρατερός	Mighty
103	μάλιστα	Most, especially
104	μέγα, μεγάλα	Greatly

105	μέλας	Dark, black
106	μέσος	Middle, the middle of
107	μηδέ	But not, nor, not even
108	νύ	Now
109	ὅθι	Where
110	οἶος	Alone
111	οἷος	Of what sort
112	ὀξύς	Sharp
113	ὅστις	Whoever
114	πάρος	Before, formerly
115	πατρίς	Native
116	πολύς	Much, many
117	πολύ	Much, very
118	πού	Anywhere, somewhere
119	πρίν	Before
120	πρῶτον, πρῶτα	First
121	πρῶτος	First
122	πτερόεις	Winged
123	πώ	Yet
124	τίς, τί	Who?
125	τῶ (τῷ)	Then, therefore
126	ὑμεῖς	You
127	ὧδε	So, thus
128	ὠκύς	Swift

129	ἀγλαός	Splendid
130	ἄγχι	Near
131	αἰγίοχος	Aegis-holding
132	αἰέν	Always, ever
133	αἰνός	Dreadful
134	αἰπύς	Steep, towering
135	ἀμείνων	Better
136	ἄμφω	Both
137	ἄντα	Opposite
138	ἀντίθεος	Godlike
139	ἀντίον	Opposite, against
140	ἀργαλέος	Hard, difficult
141	αὖθι	There, here
142	αὐτοῦ	There
143	αὔτως	Merely, as it is
144	γλαυκῶπις	Gleaming-eyed
145	γλαφυρός	Hollow
146	δαΐφρων	Fiery-hearted
147	δεινός	Dreadful
148	δεῦρο	Hither
149	διοτρεφής	Zeus-nurtured
150	εἷς	One
151	ἔισος	Equal, like
152	εἴσω	Within, into
153	ἔνδον	Within

154	ἕνεκα, εἵνεκα	On account of, for
155	ἕτερος	Other, the other
156	ζωός	Alive
157	ἠμέν	Both
158	ἡμέτερος	Our, ours
159	θεῖος	Sacred, godlike
160	ἱερός, ἱρός	Strong, sacred
161	ἶσος	Equal, like
162	κλυτός	Glorious, fine
163	κοῖλος	Hollow
164	κρείων	Ruling
165	λευκός	Clear, white
166	λυγρός	Miserable
167	μακρός	Long, tall
168	μᾶλλον	More
169	μεγάθυμος	Great-hearted
170	μεγαλήτωρ	Great-hearted, proud
171	νέος	New, young
172	νήπιος	Infant
173	νῶι	We two, both of us
174	οἴκαδε	Homeward
175	ὄπισθε, ὄπιθε	Behind
176	ὀπίσω	Backward, behind
177	ὁπότε, ὁππότε	Whenever, when
178	ὅπως, ὅππως	How, that
179	ὅτι	That, because
180	ὅτις	Whoever
181	οὐκέτι	No longer
182	οὖν	Therefore, then
183	οὕνεκα	Wherefore, because
184	οὕτως	Thus
185	πάλιν	Backwards, back
186	περικαλλής	Very beautiful

187	περίφρων	Very prudent
188	πολλόν	Much
189	πολύμητις	Crafty
190	πόποι	Alas!
191	πρό	Before, forward
192	προπάροιθε	Before, formerly
193	πρόσθεν	In front, before
194	πρότερος	Former
195	πυκινός	Close, thick
196	πως	Somehow
197	σχεδόν	Near, hard by
198	τάχα	Quickly, soon
199	ταχύς	Swift
200	τάχιστα	Most speedily
201	τὶ	Somewhat
202	τοῖος	Such, of such a kind
203	τοιοῦτος	Of such a kind, such
204	τόσσος	So great, so much
205	τόφρα	So long
206	ὑπέρ	Over, in behalf of
207	ὑψηλός	Lofty
208	φαεινός	Bright
209	φαίδιμος	Shining, illustrious
210	χαλεπός	Hard, difficult
211	χάλκεος	Brazen
212	χρύσειος	Golden
213	χρύτεος	Golden
214	ὦκα	Quickly
215	ὥς τε	As, just as

216	ἀγανός	Wondrous, illustrious
217	ἀγήνωρ	Valorous
218	ἄγριος	Wild, savage
219	ἀγχοῦ	Near, hard by
220	ἀεικής	Unseemly, disgraceful
221	ἀέκων	Unwilling
222	αἰδοῖος	Modest, respected
223	αἶθοψ	Gleaming
224	ἄκρος	Topmost, highest
225	ἀλεγεινός	Painful, toilsome
226	ἅλις	Crowded together
227	ἄλκιμος	Valiant
228	ἄλλοτε	At another time
229	ἀμβρόσιος	Ambrosial, divine
230	ἄμφις	On both sides
231	ἀντικρύ	Opposite, straight through
232	ἀντίος	Opposite
233	ἀολλής	In throngs, together
234	ἀπάνευθε	Away, apart from
235	ἀργύρεος	Of silver
236	ἀρήιος	Warlike
237	ἀρηίφιλος	Dear to Ares
238	ἄσπετος	Inexpressible, immense
239	ἆσσον	Nearer
240	ἀτάλαντος	Like, equal

241 ἀτρεκέως	Unerringly, truly
242 αὐτόθι	There, here
243 ἄφαρ	Instantly
244 ἀφνειός	Wealthy, rich in
245 βαθύς	Deep
246 βαρύς	Heavy
247 γεραιός	Old, aged
248 δειλός	Cowardly, miserable
249 δεινόν	Dreadfully
250 δεξιός	Right (hand), propitious
251 δήϊος	Blazing, hostile
252 δήν	Long, for a long time
253 δηρόν	Long, for a long time
254 διαμπερές	Through and through, forever
255 διογενής	Sprung from Zeus
256 δοιώ	Two
257 δολιχόσκιος	Long-shadowy
258 δουρικλυτός, δουρικλειτός	Renowned in the use of the spear
259 δυσμενής	Hostile
260 δώδεκα	Twelve
261 ἐγγύθεν	From near, near
262 ἐγγύς	Near
263 εἴκοσι, ἐείκοσι	Twenty
264 ἐκεῖνος	That one, he
265 ἔμπεδος	Firm, unshaken
266 ἔμπης	Wholly, nevertheless
267 ἔνθεν	Thence, then, whence
268 ἐννοσίγαιος	Earth-shaking
269 ἐνοσίχθων	Earth-shaking
270 ἔντοσθε	Within
271 ἐπήν	When, after
272 ἐτέρωθεν	On the other side
273 εὐκνήμις	Well-greaved

274	ἐυκτίμενος	Well-built, well-tilled
275	εὐπλόκαμος	Fair-tressed
276	ἐύς, ἠύς	Good, noble
277	ἐύσσελμος	Well-decked
278	εὖτε	When, as
279	ἕως, εἵως, εἷος	As long as, until
280	ἡδύς	Sweet
281	ἦμος	When
282	ἤν	If
283	ἤπιος	Mild
284	ἠριγένεια	Early-born
285	ἦτε	Or, than
286	ἠύτε	As
287	θαλερός	Swelling, blooming
288	θεοειδής	Godlike
289	θεσπέσιος	Divinely uttered, divine
290	θνητός	Mortal
291	θοῦρος	Impetuous
292	θύραζε	Forth, out
293	ἰδέ	And
294	ἰθύς	Straight
295	ἱππόδαμος	Horse-taming
296	ἴφθιμος	Mighty
297	καρπαλίμως	Swiftly
298	καρτερός	Mighty, stern
299	κερδίων	Better
300	κομόωντε	Long-haired
301	κορυθαίολος	With glancing helm
302	κυδάλιμος	Glorious, noble
303	λευκώλενος	White-armed
304	λίην	Too, excessively
305	μάκαρ	Blessed
306	μακρόν, μακρά	Far, afar

307	μαλακός	Soft, gentle
308	μέγιστος	Greatest
309	μείζων	Greater
310	μειλίχιος	Mild, pleasant
311	μετόπισθε	Behind
312	μήτε	Neither, nor
313	μοῦνος	Alone
314	μυρίος	Countless
315	μῶνυξ	Single-hoofed
316	νέον	Just now, lately
317	νηλεής, νηλής	Pitiless
318	νημερτής	Unerring
319	νόσφι	Apart, aloof from, except
320	ξανθός	Yellow, blond
321	ὄβριμος	Heavy, mighty
322	ὀλίγος	Little
323	ὀλοός	Destructive
324	ὁμοῖος	Like, equal
325	ὁμῶς	Together, alike
326	ὅσον	As much as, as far as
327	πάγχυ	Altogether
328	πάμπαν	Altogether
329	πάντῃ	On all sides
330	παντοῖος	Of all sorts
331	πάντοσε	In every direction
332	πάροιθε	Before
333	παχύς	Thick
334	πεζός	On foot
335	πίων	Fat, fertile
336	πλέων (πλείων)	More, greater
337	πλεῖστος	Most, a great many
338	ποδώκης	Fleet-footed
339	ποικίλος	Varied
340	πολιός	Gray, hoary

341	πολύτλας	Much-enduring
342	πορφύρεος	Purple
343	πρόφρων	Cheerful, zealous
344	πρυμνός	Extreme, at the end of
345	πυκνός	Close, thick
346	πῶς	How?
347	ῥεῖα, ῥέα	Easily
348	ῥοδοδάκτυλος	Rosy-fingered
349	σιωπῇ	Silently
350	σμερδαλέον	Terribly
351	στιβαρός	Compact, strong
352	στυγερός	Hateful
353	σχέτλιος	Enduring, hard
354	τεός	Thy, thine
355	τῇ	Here, where
356	τῆλε	Far, far away
357	τίπτε	Why pray?
358	τοιόσδε	Such
359	τόσσον	So much
360	τούνεκα	Therefore
361	τρεῖς	Three
362	τρίς	Thrice
363	ὕπερθε	From above, above
364	ὑπέρθυμος	High spirited
365	ὑπερφίαλος	Mighty, arrogant
366	ὑπόδρα	Sternly, darkly
367	φέρτερος	Better, braver
368	φίλτατος	Dearest
369	χάλκειος	Brazen
370	χαλκήρης	Bronze-shod
371	χαλκοχίτων	Bronze-clad
372	χαμᾶζε	To the ground, down
373	ὡσεί	As if
374	ὥς περ	Just as

List XVIII
Pronouns, Adjectives, Adverbs, Prepositions, Etc., Occurring 10–25 Times

375	ἆ	Ah!
376	ἄαπτος	Invincible
377	ἀγακλειτός	Renowned
378	ἀγανός	Gentle
379	ἀγχίμολος	Near, coming near
380	ἀδινός	Thick
381	ἀεικέλιος	Unseemly, disgraceful
382	ἀέκητι	Against the will of
383	ἀθρόος	Together, in crowds
384	αἰειγενέτης	Immortal
385	αἰζηός	Vigorous
386	αἴθε	Would that
387	αἰθόμενος	Burning, blazing
388	αἴθων	Shining
389	αἱματόεις	Bloody
390	αἰνότατος	Most dreadful
391	αἰπεινός	Steep, towering
392	αἴσιμος	Destined, due
393	αἴτιος	Guilty, to blame
394	ἀκάματος	Untiring
395	ἀκαχμένος	Sharpened, pointed
396	ἀκέων	Silent, quiet
397	ἀκήν	Silently, silent
398	ἀκρότατος	Topmost, uttermost
399	ἄκων	Javelin

400	ἅλιος	Of the sea
401	ἅλιος	Fruitless, vain
402	ἄλλῃ	Elsewhere, another way
403	ἀλλοδαπός	Strange, foreign
404	ἄλλοθεν	From elsewhere
405	ἀλλότριος	Of another, strange
406	ἄλλυδις	To another place
407	ἄλλως	Otherwise
408	ἄμβροτος	Immortal
409	ἀμήχανος	Helpless, impossible
410	ἄμυδις	Together, at once
411	ἀμφιγυήεις	Strong in both arms
412	ἀμφιέλισσα	Curved at both ends
413	ἀμφικύπελλον	Double-cupped
414	ἀμφοτέρωθεν	On both sides
415	ἀναιδής	Shameless, pitiless
416	ἄναλκις	Cowardly
417	ἀνδροφόνος	Man-slaying
418	ἄνευθε	Away, apart
419	ἄντην	Opposite, in front
420	ἀντί	Against, instead of
421	ἀντία	Opposite, against
422	ἄξιος	Of equal weight, worth
423	ἁπαλός	Tender
424	ἀπείρων	Boundless
425	ἀπερείσιος	Boundless
426	ἀπήμων	Unharmed
427	ἀπηνής	Unfeeling, harsh
428	ἀργιόδους	White-toothed
429	ἀργυρόηλος	Silver-studded
430	ἀργυρόπεζα	Silver-footed
431	ἀργυρότοξος	With silver bow
432	ἀρείων	Better

433	ἀριστερός	Left, ill-boding
434	ἀρνειός	Ram
435	ἄρσην	Male
436	ἀσάμινθος	Bath-tub
437	ἄσβεστος	Inextinguishable
438	ἀσπάσιος	Welcome, glad
439	ἀσπασίως	Gladly
440	ἀστερόεις	Starry
441	ἀτάσθαλος	Wicked, wanton
442	ἀτειρής	Unwearied
443	ἄτερ	Without, apart from
444	ἀτρύγετος	Barren
445	αὔριον	To-morrow
446	ἄφρων	Thoughtless, foolish
447	βόειος	Of an ox, of oxen
448	βουληφόρος	Counselling
449	βοῶπις	Ox-eyed
450	βροτολοιγός	Man-destroying
451	γαιήοχος	Earth-holding
452	γλυκερός	Sweet
453	γλυκύς	Sweet
454	γναμπτός	Bent
455	γνωτός	Known, related
456	γυμνός	Naked, unarmed
457	δαιδάλεος	Skilfully wrought
458	δαιμόνιος	Possessed
459	δακρυόεις	Weeping
460	δέκα	Ten
461	δέκατος	Tenth
462	δεξιτερός	Right (hand)
463	δεύτερον	Secondly, again
464	δεύτερος	Second, next
465	δηθά	Long, a long time

466	διίφιλος	Dear to Zeus
467	δίκαιος	Right, just
468	δινήεις	Eddying
469	δίχα	In two
470	δολιχός	Long
471	δυοκαίδεκα	Twelve
472	δύστηνος	Unhappy
473	ἐγγύθι	Near
474	εἴκελος	Like
475	εἰλίπος	Close-footed, trailing-footed
476	ἐκάεργος	Far-working
477	ἐκάς	Far, far from
478	ἐκάτερθε	On both sides
479	ἔκηλος	Of good cheer, at ease
480	ἐκτός	Outside, outside of
481	ἔκτοσθε	Outside, outside of
482	ἐκών	Willing, of one's own will
483	ἕλιξ	Bent, crook-horned
484	ἔμπεδον	Firmly
485	ἐναίσιμος	Fateful, favorable, proper
486	ἐναλίγκιος	Like
487	ἐναντίβιον	With hostile front against
488	ἐναντίον	Opposite, against
489	ἐναντίος	Opposite, against
490	ἐνδόθι	Within
491	ἐνδυκέως	Duly, kindly
492	ἐννέα	Nine
493	ἐννῆμαρ	For nine days
494	ἐντός	Within
495	ἕξ	Six
496	ἐξαπίνης	Suddenly
497	ἐξαῦτις	Again, anew
498	ἐξείης	In order

499	ἔξοχον, ἔξοχα	Chiefly, by far
500	ἔξοχος	Pre-eminent
501	ἐπιείκελος	Like
502	ἐπιεικής	Suitable
503	ἐπισταμένως	Skilfully
504	ἐπιχθόνιος	Earthly, upon earth
505	ἑπτά	Seven
506	ἐρατεινός	Lovely
507	ἐριβῶλαξ	With large clods, fertile
508	ἐρίγδουπος, ἐρίδουπος	Resounding
509	ἐρίηρος	Trusty
510	ἐρικυδής	Glorious
511	ἐρυθρός	Red
512	ἐσσυμένως	Hastily
513	ἐτεόν	Truly, truth
514	ἑτέρωσε	In the other direction
515	ἐτήτυμον	Actually, really
516	ἑτοῖμος	Ready
517	ἐΰδμητος	Well-built
518	εὐεργής	Well-made
519	ἐΰξεστος	Well-scraped, polished
520	ἐΰξοος	Well-polished
521	εὐρυάγυιος	Wide-streeted
522	εὐρύοπα	Wide-thundering
523	εὐρύχορος	With broad lawns
524	ἐΰτυκτος	Well-wrought
525	ζείδωρος	Grain-giving
526	ἠγάθεος	Sacred
527	ἠεροειδής	Misty, dim
528	ἠμαθόεις	Sandy
529	ἥμισυς	Half
530	ἠνεμόεις	Windy
531	ἠΰκομος	Fair-haired

532	ἠῶθεν	In the morning
533	θαρσαλέος	Daring, bold
534	θᾶσσον	More speedily
535	θερμός	Warm
536	θέσφατος	Divinely decreed, divine
537	θῆλυς	Female
538	θήν	Doubtless
539	θοῶς	Swiftly
540	θρασύς	Bold, daring
541	θυμαλγής	Heart-grieving
542	ἴκελος	Like, resembling
543	ἱμερόεις	Passionate, fond, lovely
544	ἶος	One
545	ἰοχέαιρα	Pouring arrows
546	ἱππόβοτος	Horse-breeding
547	ἰσόθεος	Godlike
548	ἶσον, ἶσα	Equally
549	ἶφι	With might
550	ἴφιος	Strong, goodly
551	ἰχθυόεις	Abounding in fish
552	καθύπερθε	From above
553	κακῶς	Badly
554	καλλίθριξ	With beautiful mane, fair-fleeced
555	καλλιπάρῃος	Fair-cheeked
556	κάλλιστος	Fairest
557	καλλίων	Fairer
558	καλόν	Finely
559	καμπύλος	Bent, curved
560	κάρτιστος	Mightiest, best
561	καταθνητός	Mortal
562	κεδνός	Careful, good
563	κεῖθεν	Thence, then
564	κεῖθι	There

565	κεῖσε	Thither
566	κελαινεφής	Of dark clouds, dark
567	κελαινός	Dark, black
568	κλειτός	Famous
569	κολλητός	Joined, shod
570	κορωνίς	Curved
571	κουρίδιος	Wedded
572	κραιπνός	Quick, hasty
573	κραταιός	Mighty
574	κρατερῶς	Mightily
575	κρείσσων	Stronger, better
576	κυάνεος	Dark blue, dark
577	κυανόπρῳρος	Dark-prowed
578	κύδιστος	Most glorious
579	λάθρῃ	Secretly
580	λαιψηρός	Nimble, swift
581	λεπτός	Peeled, fine, delicate
582	λευγαλέος	Mournful
583	λιγύς	Clear, loud
584	λιπαρός	Shining, rich
585	μάν	Verily, indeed
586	μείλινος	Ashen
587	μελιηδής	Honey-sweet
588	μελίφρων	Honey-minded, sweet
589	μενεπτόλεμος	Steadfast in battle
590	μενοεικής	Grateful, satisfying
591	μέροψ	Mortal
592	μεσσηγύ(s)	In the middle, between
593	μηκέτι	No longer, no more
594	μήν	Indeed
595	μίννυνθα	For a little, a little while
596	ναί	Yea
597	νείατος	Newest, last

598	νέρθε	Below, under
599	νεώτερος	Newer, under
600	νόθος	Illegitimate
601	νόστιμος	Of return
602	ξεινήιος	Of friendship
603	ξεστός	Scraped, polished
604	ὅθεν	Whence
605	ὀιζυρός	Wretched
606	οἶνοψ	Wine-colored
607	οἶον	As, how
608	ὄλβιος	Happy, blessed
609	ὀλίγον	A little
610	ὀμηγερής	Assembled, together
611	ὁμοίιος	Like, equal
612	ὁμοῦ	Together
613	ὀμφαλόεις	Studded, bossed
614	ὀξύ	Sharply, piercingly
615	ὀξυόεις	Sharp-pointed
616	ὅπῃ	Where, as
617	ὁππότερος	Whichever
618	ὀρθός	Upright, erect
619	οὐδείς	No one, nothing
620	οὐλόμενος	Destructive, accursed
621	οὖλος	Thick, woolly
622	οὐρανίων	Heavenly
623	οὐρανόθεν	From heaven
624	ὄχ(α)	By far
625	ὀψέ	Late
626	παιπαλόεις	Rugged, rough
627	πάλαι	Long ago
628	παλαιός	Ancient, old
629	πανημέριος	All day long
630	παννύχιος	All night long

631	παρέκ, παρέξ	Along past, close by
632	πατρώιος	Paternal, hereditary
633	παῦρος	Little, few
634	πελώριος	Monstrous, huge
635	πεντήκοντα	Fifty
636	πέπων	Ripe, dear, coward
637	περικλυτός	Renowned
638	πετεηνός	Winged, fledged
639	πῇ, πῆ	Whither? how?
640	πή, πή	Anywhere, in any way
641	πικρός	Sharp, bitter
642	πιστός	Trusty, faithful
643	πλεῖος	Full
644	πλείων	More, greater
645	πλησίον	Near, hard by
646	πλησίος	Near, neighboring
647	ποδάρκης	Swift-footed
648	ποδήνεμος	Wind-swift
649	πόθεν	Whence?
650	ποθέν	From somewhere
651	ποθί	At some time, somewhere
652	ποιητός	Made, built
653	ποῖος	Of what sort?
654	πολλάκις	Often
655	πολυδαίδαλος	Much wrought, skilful
656	πολυμήχανος	Much contriving, ever ready
657	πολύφρων	Very sagacious
658	ποντοπόρος	Sea-traversing
659	ποῦ	Where? Whither?
660	πουλυβότειρα	All-nourishing
661	πρηνής	On the face, head foremost
662	πρόπας	All, all together
663	πρόσ(σ)ω	Forward, in the future

664	προτέρω	Forward, further
665	πρώτιστος	First of all
666	πτολίπορθος	City-sacking
667	πτωχός	Poor, beggar
668	πύκα	Thickly, carefully
669	πυκινῶς	Close, fast
670	πύματος	Last
671	ῥηιδίως	Easily
672	ῥίμφα	Swiftly
673	σάφα	Clearly
674	σήμερον	Today
675	σιγαλόεις	Shining
676	σιγῇ	Silently
677	σιδήρεος	Of iron
678	σκιόεις	Shady, shadowy
679	σμερδαλέος	Fearful
680	σόος	Safe
681	σῶς	Safe, certain
682	στονόεις	Mournful, grievous
683	σφέτερος	Their
684	σφός	Their
685	ταλασίφρων	Stout-hearted
686	ταχύπωλος	With swift steeds
687	τέρην	Tender
688	τερπικέραυνος	Delighting in thunder
689	τεσσαράκοντα	Forty
690	τέσσαρες	Four
691	τέως, τείως, τεῖος	So long, meanwhile
692	τηλόθεν	From far
693	τηλόθι	Far away
694	τηλοῦ	Afar, far from
695	τοιγάρ	Accordingly
696	τοῖον	So

697	τοσόσδε	So great, so much
698	τρηχύς	Rough, rugged
699	τρίτατος	Third
700	τρίτος	Third
701	τυτθόν, τυτθά	Little, a little
702	τυτθός	Little, small
703	ὑγρός	Moist, wet
704	ὑλήεις	Wooded
705	ὑμέτερος	Your, yours
706	ὕπατος	Highest, supreme
707	ὑπένερθε	Beneath, below
708	ὑπερηνορέων	Haughty
709	ὑπερμενής	High-spirited
710	ὕπτιος	Back, on the back
711	ὕστατον, ὕστατα	Last
712	ὕστερον	Later
713	ὑψερεφής	High-roofed
714	ὕψοσε	Upward, aloft
715	φέρτατος	Best, bravest
716	φιλοπτόλεμος	Fond of war
717	χαμάδις	To the ground
718	χαμαί	On the ground
719	χαρίεις	Pleasing, graceful
720	χείρων	Worse, inferior
721	χερείων	Worse, inferior
722	χλωρός	Green, yellow
723	χρυσόθρονος	Golden-throned
724	ὠκύπορος	Swift-sailing
725	ὠκύπος	Swift-footed

INDEX TO VERBS

The numbers following the index entries refer to the frequency listing of the verbs on pages 3–22.

Disobey, 179
Distress, 168, 231
Distribute, 96, 129
Divide, 195
Divine, 425
Do, sacrifice, 105
Drag, 102, 361
Draw, 52, 328
Dread, fear, 43
Drink, 140
Drive, strike, 205
Dwell, inhabit, 68
Eager, press on, 66
Eat, 99, 217, 375
Empty, sack, 301
Enchant, 387
Encounter, 308–310
Encourage, 385
End, 81, 277
Endure, 154, 507
Enjoin, charge, 152
Enrage, anger, 160
Enter, 46, 201
Equip, prepare, 257
Escape notice, 240
Excel, 395
Exchange, 15
Exhaust, 511
Fall, 30
Fasten, hold, 93
Favor, 288
Feed, pasture, 335
Fetter, 462
Fight, 65, 122, 123
Fill, 139
Find, 108, 116
Fit, 94
Fix, build, 268
Flay, 347

Flee, 32, 508, 515
Flight, 284
Fling, hurl, 479
Flow, 146, 374, 436
Fly, 138
Fold, 473
Force, 333
Frequent, 476
Gather, tell, 63
Gaze at, 388
Gird, 380
Give, 4, 144, 287, 290
Go, 2, 6, 60, 69, 372, 441, 520
Going, about, 124
Grieve, 95, 329
Groan, lament, 274
Grow, 286, 293
Grudge, deny, 519
Guide, lead, 219
Hand over, 356
Harangue, speak, 35
Harm, slay, 349
Hate, 378
Have, 9, 430, 525
Heal, 300
Hear, 37, 299
Heard, cry out, 338
Hearken, 61
Heavy, charge, 337
Help, 451, 524
Hide, 230, 412
Hit, happen, 281
Hold, 106, 113, 523
Hope, 103
Hurl, 169
Impede, harm, 334
Increase, 457
Kill, 23, 156

Kindle, blaze, 194
King (am), 92, 332
Kiss, 414
Knock, smite, 234
Know, 26, 41, 211
Labor, 271, 466
Lack, 197
Lament, 131
Lash, whip, 427
Laugh, 190
Lead, 1
Leader, command, 218
Lean, press, 213
Lean, sink, 118
Leap, 91, 221
Learn, 145
Leave, 24
Let, let go, 20, 47
Lie, 22, 422
Like (am), befit, 51
Live, 109
Loathe, hate, 494
Look, see, 346
Loose, release, 64
Lord, rule, 406
Lose, destroy, 27, 447
Love, 158
Mad, rage, 423
Make, 12, 83, 142, 316, 362, 368, 468, 490
March, move, 489
Marry, 188
Meet, 307, 311
Melt, 502
Miss, 120, 175, 469
Mix, 127, 399
Move, 19, 402, 481
Moved, vexed, 264
Mow, reap, 305

Suffer, 74
Supplicate, 340
Swim, 438
Take, 14, 62, 180, 416
Take a meal, 344
Taken, captured, 304
Take oath, 256
Talk, speak, 331
Tame, subdue, 343
Taste, enjoy, 461
Taunt, tease, 400
Teach, 193, 351
Test, 463
Think, 72, 88, 199
Threaten, 178
Throng, go, 448
Throw, smite, 3
Thrust, 161

Thunder, 200
Toil, suffer, 247
Tremble, dread, 510
Troubled, 289, 501
Try, 136
Turn, 85, 149, 419, 493, 512
Urge, 59, 73
Utter, speak, 517
Value, honor, 153
Wail, 192, 415
Wait, convey, 233
Wander, rove, 170
War, 143
Warm, delight, 391
Wash, 439, 440
Waste, 157, 518
Watch, guard, 285

Wear, out, 276
Weave, 513
Wed, 455
Weep, 117
Wet, moisten, 348
Whirl, 354
Will, wish, 18, 187
Wipe away, 450
Wish to sleep, 398
Wonder, 220, 382
Wont, 358
Woo, 246
Work, 79, 228, 322
Wrap, envelop, 360
Wroth, 432
Yield, 203
Yoke, 379

INDEX TO NOUNS

The numbers following the index entries refer to the frequency of the nouns on pages 23–44.

Courage, 388
Courtyard, 175
Cow, ox, 39
Crash, thunder, 433
Crest, 229, 444
Cry, 176, 394
Cup, 434
Dance, place, 566
Darkness, 383, 421, 531
Dawn, morning, 48
Day, 46
Death, 50, 103
Deceit, 192
Deck, ribs, 397
Defense, valor, 80
Depth, 333
Desire, wish, 364
Destruction, 120, 443
Diaphragm, 29, 511
Din, 354, 482, 491
Dismissal, 262
Ditch, 279
Divinity, 90
Dog, 56
Door, gate, 101
Doorway, porch, 512
Dream, 488
Drink, 263, 510
Dust, ashes, 107
Eagle, 303
Ear, 256
Earth, 8, 143, 157, 257, 339
Effort, 532
End, 280, 501
Erinys, 373
Escort, 509
Estate, 542
Evil, 222

Excellence, 168
Eye, 64, 123, 485
Eyelid, 179
Face, 513
Falsehood, 571
Family, race, 184
Fat, 351
Fate, 264, 480
Father, 25
Fatigue, toil, 223
Fawn, 467
Fear, 348
Feast, 91
Feather, wing, 515
Female, slave, 94
Fetter, 189
Field, country, 152
Fight, 57
Fire, 68
Fish, 403
Flame, blaze, 554
Fleece, 435
Flesh, meat, 233
Flight, 291
Flock, 516
Flood, stream, 524
Folly, 326
Food, 194, 363, 365
Foot, 28
Foot-stool, 391
Force, violence, 38
Forehead, 457
Form, 556
Fortune, 481
Frame, build, 188
Fruit, grain, 409
Gain, 417
Gall, wrath, 146
Garment, 95, 518

Gate, 131
Gift, 44, 185, 474
Girdle, 384
Girl, 54
Gleam, 327, 526
Glen, ravine, 334
Glory, 110, 379
Goat, 78
Goat-herd, 305
Goblet, 92
God, 2
Goddess, 51
Gold, 148
Grace, charm, 561
Groaning, 534
Ground, 344
Guide, leader, 207
Gust, 301
Hair, 392, 426, 560
Hall, 19
Hand, 6
Handmaid, 81
Harbor, 238
Head, 52, 102, 232, 408
Head-band, 428
Heap, strand, 214
Heart, 3, 97, 104, 108
Hearth, 376
Heaven, 124
Hecatomb, 197
Hedge, court, 204
Helmet, 228, 547
Help, helper, 201, 486
Herald, 105
Herb, drug, 288
Herdsman, 336
Hero, warrior, 47
Hog, 527
Holder, 494

Rope, arms, 490
Row, rank, 277
Rug, 521, 538
Ruin, folly, 174
Ruler, 239
Rumor, glory, 106
Runner, guide, 352
Rush, sweep, 374
Sacrifice, 219
Sail, 402
Sailor, 466
Salt, sea, 33
Sand, 570
Sandals, 500
Savor, fat, 423
Scale, talent, 536
Sea, 49, 66
Season, time, 296
Seat, 361, 362
Seer, 449
Shame, respect, 158
Shape, phantom, 366
Sheep, 112, 118
Shepherd, 127, 472
Shield, 83, 132
Shin, 422
Ship, 4
Shoot, twig, 477
Shore, 308, 386
Shoulder, 76
Shout, 86
Sigh, token, 133
Silver, 321
Sinew, 220, 468
Sister, 412
Skin, 75, 349, 522
Sky, 159
Slave, 191
Sleep, 74, 424

Smoke, 406
Son, 5
Song, 164
Son-in-law, 338
Space, place, 295
Spear, lance, 13
Spearman, 162
Spit, 476
Spoils, 371
Spring, 429
Staff, scepter, 274
Stag, 368
Star, 325
Stature, 451
Step, altar, 337
Stern-cable, 514
Stone, 237, 436, 564
Stone, 436, 564
Stranger, 23
Strap, 398, 541
Stream, 271, 519
Strength, 231, 272
Strife, 203
Suitor, 21
Sun, 45
Supper, 193
Suppliant, 396
Surf, 520
Sweat, 395
Swine, 137, 551
Swineherd, 136, 552
Sword, 116, 290, 319
Table, 283
Tear, 41
Tempest, 437
Temple, 470
Temple (human), 430
Thigh, 240
Thigh-pieces, 460

Thought, plan, 471
Threshing-floor, 313
Threshold, 258
Throng, 121
Thunder-bolt, 416
Tidings, 150
Time, 294
Tin, 413
Tongue, language, 340
Tooth, 248
Torch, 343
Tower, 269
Town, citadel, 267
Treasure, 414
Tree, 347, 356
Trembling, 545
Tripod, 284
Tunic, 144
Usage, justice, 353
Vagabond, 310
Victory, 245
Voice, 259, 293, 328
Wagon, 314, 320
Wall, 70, 544
Want, need, 567, 568
War, battle, 26, 266
Warrior, 324, 508
Watchman, 530
Water, 73
Wave, 55
Way, journey, 117
Wheat, food, 134
Whip, 450
Wife, 32, 307, 497
Will, 400
Wind, 34, 180, 382, 473, 492
Wine, 63
Witness, oath, 252

INDEX TO PRONOUNS, ADJECTIVES, ADVERBS, ETC.

The numbers following the index entries refer to the frequency listing of pronouns, adjectives, adverbs, etc., on pages 45–70.

Here, where, 355
Highest, 706
High-roofed, 713
High-spirited, 709
Him, her, it, 28, 34
His, her, own, 57
Hither, here, 95, 148
Hollow, 145, 163
Homeward, 174
Honey-sweet, 587, 588
Horse-breeding, 546
Horse-taming, 295
Hostile, 259, 487
How(?) 66, 178, 346
I, 10
If, 11, 81, 282
Illegitimate, 600
Immortal, 384, 408
Impetuous, 291
In, 14
Indeed, 9, 26, 594
Inexpressible, 238
Inextinguishable, 437
Infant, 172
In order, 498
Instantly, 243
Into, 12
In truth; pray?, 19
Invincible, 376
Iron (of), 677
Javelin, 399
Joined, shod, 569
Just as, 374
Known, 455
Last, 670, 711
Late(r), 625, 712
Lawns (with), 523
Left, ill, 433
Like, 240, 324, 474, 486,

501, 542, 611
Little, 322, 595, 609, 633,
    701, 702
Lofty, 207
Long, 167, 470; ago, 627;
    time, 252, 253, 465
Long-haired, 300
Long-shadowy, 257
Lovely, 506
Made, built, 652
Male, 435
Man-destroying, 450
Man-slaying, 417
Merely, as is, 143
Middle, 106, 592
Might(y) 102, 296, 298,
    365, 549, 560, 573, 574
Mild, 283, 310
Miserable, 166
Misty, dim, 527
Modest, respected, 222
Moist, wet, 703
Monstrous, 634
More, 168, 336, 644
Morning, 532
Mortal, 93, 290, 561, 591
Most, 103, 337
Mournful, 582, 682
Much, 39, 116, 117, 188
My, mine, 56
Naked, 456
Near, 130, 197, 219, 239,
    261, 262, 379, 473,
    645, 646
Native, 115
Neither, nor, 68, 312
New, young, 171
Newer, under, 599
Newest, last, 597

Nimble, swift, 580
Nine, 492; days, 493
No longer, 181, 593
No one, nothing, 619
Nor, not even, 35
Not, 27, 33
Nourishing, 660
Now, 29, 108, 316
O, oh!, 79
Often, 654
Of what sort, 111, 653
Old, aged, 247
On account of, 154
On both sides, 47
One, 150, 544
One another, 84
On foot, 334
Opposite, 137, 139, 231,
    232, 419, 421, 488,
    489
Or, than, 18, 285
Other, 2, 155
Other direction, 514
Other side, 272
Otherwise, 407
Our, ours, 158
Out, out of, 13
Outside, 480, 481
Over, 206
Ox, of oxen, 447
Ox-eyed, 449
Painful, 225
Passionate, 543
Paternal, 632
Peeled, 581
Pitiless, 317
Pleasing, 719
Poor, beggar, 667
Possessed, 458

Under, 78
Unerring(ly), 241, 318
Unfeeling, 427
Unhappy, 472
Unharmed, 426
Unseemly, 220, 381
Untiring, 394
Unwearied, 442
Unwilling, 221
Up, 49
Upon, on, 17
Upright, erect, 618
Upward, aloft, 714
Valiant, 227
Valorous, 217
Varied, 339
Verily, indeed, 585
Very, 24, 38
Vigorous, 385
Warlike, 236
Warm, 535
We, 61; both, 173
Wealthy, 244
Wedded, 571
Weeping, 459

Welcome, glad, 438
Well, 60
Well-built, 274, 517
Well-decked, 277
Well-greaved, 273
Well-made, 518
Well-polished, 520
Well-scraped, 519
Well-wrought, 524
When, 16, 32, 271, 278, 281
Whence, 604, 649
Whenever, when, 177
Where, 100, 109, 616, 659
Wherefore, 183
Whichever, 617
While, until, 70
White-armed, 303
White-toothed, 428
Whither?, how?, 639
Who, 67, 124
Whoever, 113, 180
Wholly, 266
Why, pray?, 357

Wicked, 441
Wide-streeted, 521
Wide-thundering, 522
Wild, savage, 218
Willing, 482
Wind-swift, 648
Windy, 530
Wine-colored, 606
Winged, 122, 638
With bow, 431
Within, 152, 153, 270, 490, 494
Without, 443
Wondrous, 216
Wooded, 704
Worse, 720, 721
Would that, 386
Wretched, 605
Wrought, 457, 655
Yea, 596
Yellow, blond, 320
Yet, 123
You, 126
Your, yours, 705
Zeus-nurtured, 149